BOOK 2

Especially in *Romantic Style*

8 Lyrical Solos for Intermediate Pianist

Dennis Alexander

D1408380

Music written in romantic style is instantly appealing and some of the most accessible in terms of interpretation. Much of the music from the Romantic era was written especially for the piano. *Especially in Romantic Style* was written for pianists who love the expressive qualities of this instrument and the sounds of the romantic style. The warm, lyrical melodies and the rich harmonies of these pieces will appeal to pianists of any age. Through this music, students can learn to play with a beautiful tone, listen to each note, and shape musical phrases, preparing them to study the great Romantic period piano masterpieces of Chopin, Mendelssohn and Schumann. It is my hope that each of these musical vignettes will inspire students to create a beautiful sound and to play with expressiveness, musicality and finesse.

With all best wishes,

Dennis Alexander

This collection is dedicated to my friend and colleague, Amy Greer.

Copyright © MMIX by Alfred Music Publishing Co., Inc.
All rights reserved.   Printed in USA.
ISBN-10: 0-7390-6092-9
ISBN-13: 978-0-7390-6092-6

Alfred

Forest Whispers

Dennis Alexander

Boston Blues

Dennis Alexander

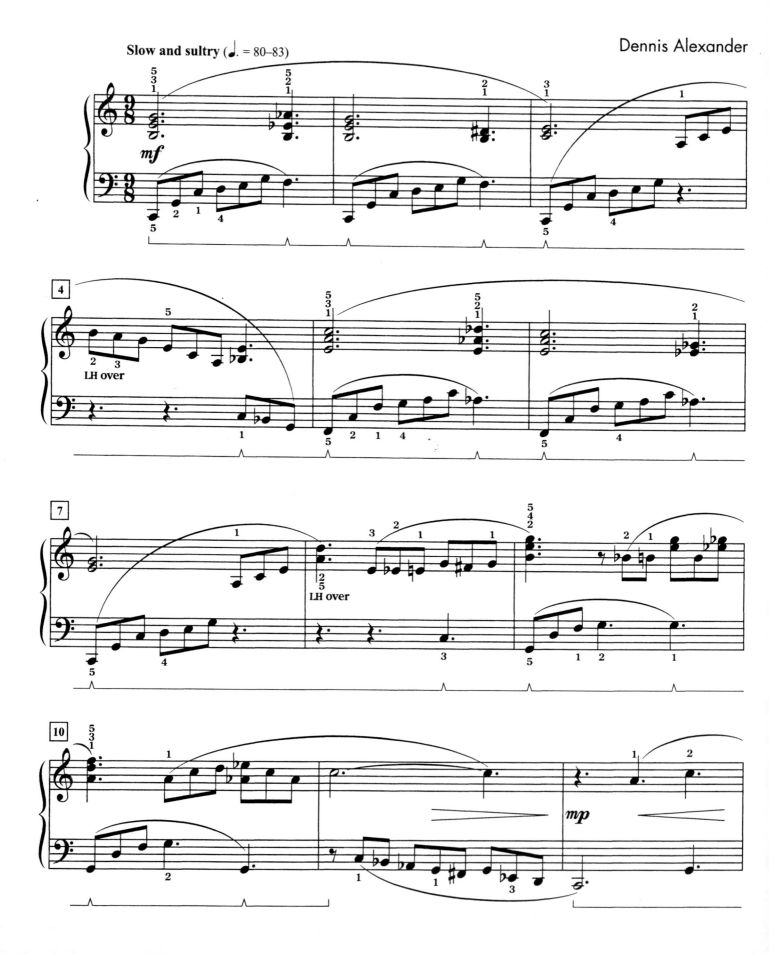

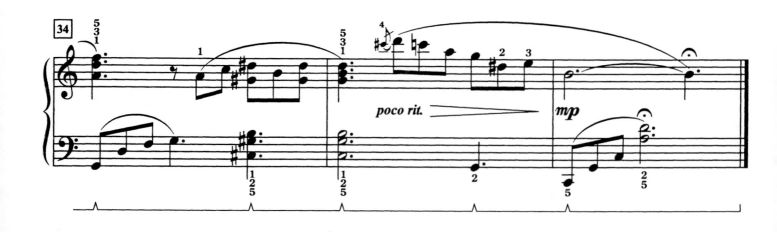

Enchanted Moments

Dennis Alexander

Tone Painting No. 1

Dennis Alexander

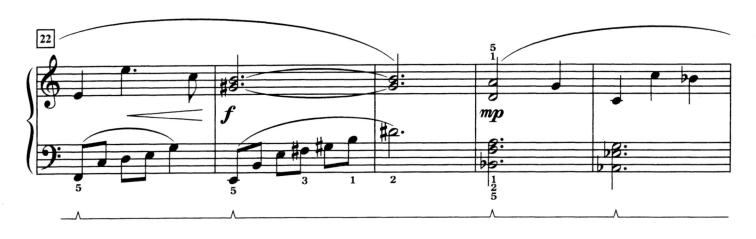

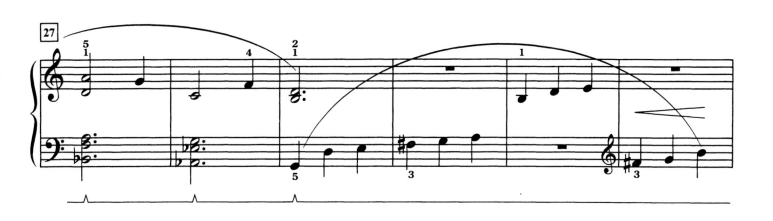

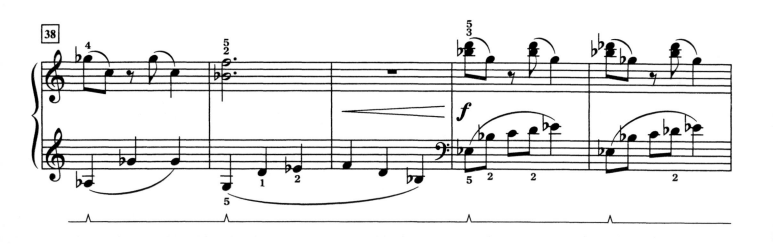

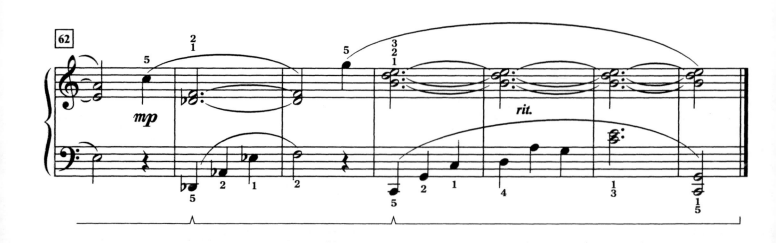

Winter Dreams

Dennis Alexander

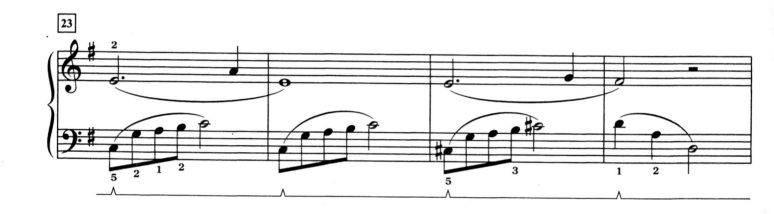

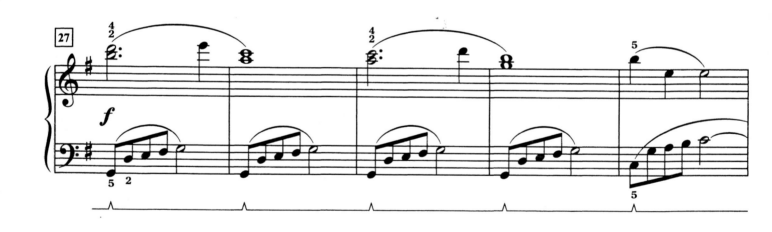

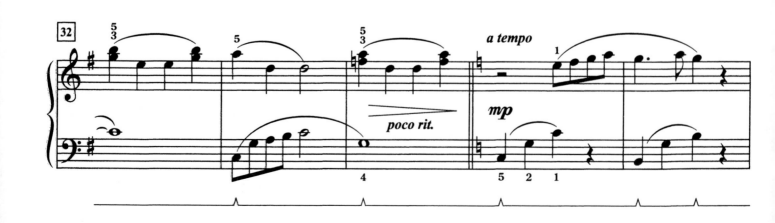

Jazz Romance

Dennis Alexander

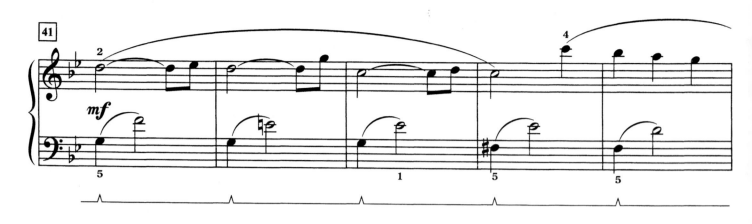

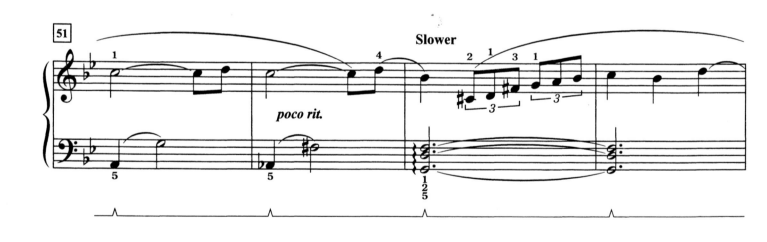

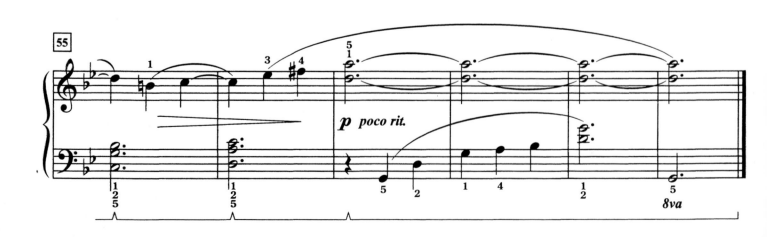

Impromptu in G Minor

Dennis Alexander

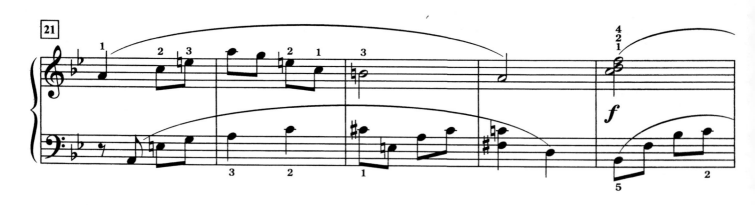

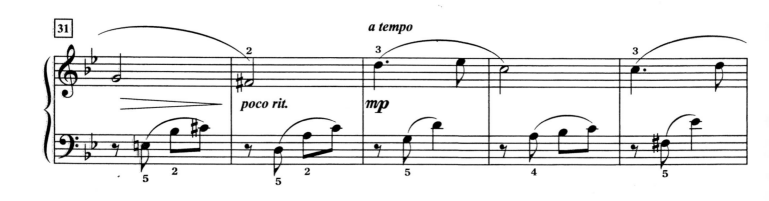

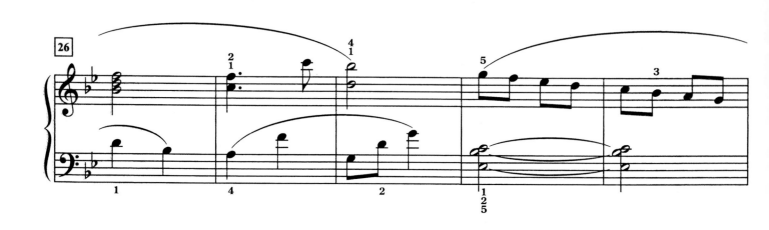

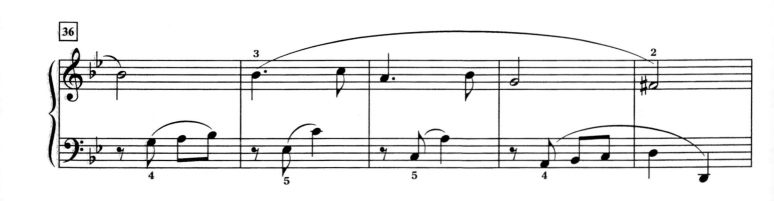

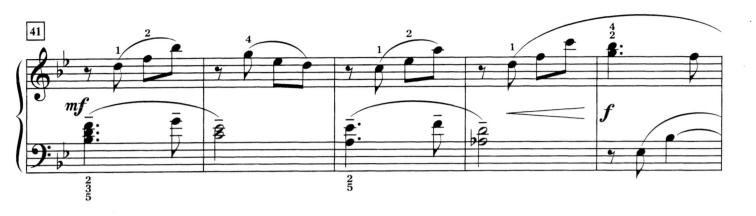

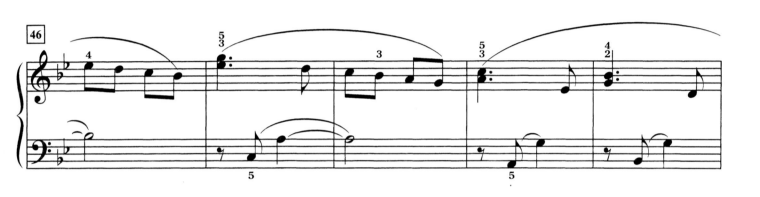

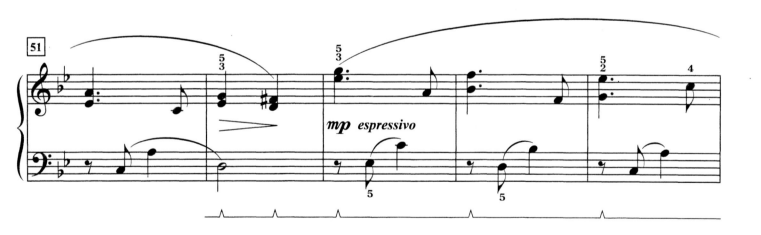

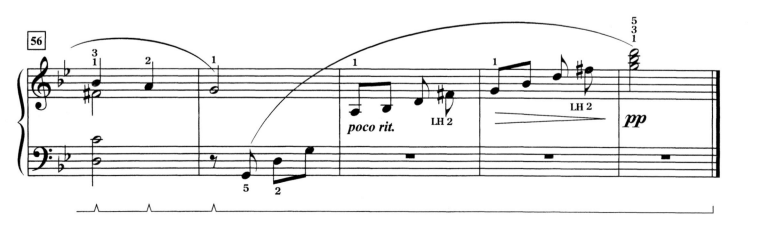

Arioso in D Major

Dennis Alexander